S0-CFI-774

MERLION ARTS LIBRARY

BEATING THE DRUM

by Josephine Paker

Merlion Publishing

First published 1992 by
Merlion Publishing Ltd
2 Bellinger Close
Greenways Business Park
Chippenham
Wiltshire SN15 1BN
UK

2nd printing 1993

Consultant: Denys Darlow F.R.C.M., F.L.C.M.
Designer: Tracy Carrington

Printed in Great Britain by BPCC Paulton Books

ISBN 1 85737 038 4

Cover photography by Mike Stannard.

Artwork on pages 6, 14, 19 and 35 by Kevin Kimber; pages 16—17 and 32 by Kiki Lewis and pages 7, 8—9, 12—13, 25, 26, 28, 32, 37, 38—39 and 41 by Andrew Midgley.

Models on pages 5, 11, 21 and 39 by Tracy Carrington.

Photographs on pages 5, 8, 10—11, 12—13, 17, 20—21, 22—23, 27, 31, 33, 34—35, 37, 39, 41 and 42—43 by Mike Stannard.

CONTENTS

What is percussion?

A drummer playing at a wedding in southern India

Listen to the noises around you. Can you hear a ticking clock, a radio playing or the hum of a car engine? Thousands of years ago, people listened to the sounds around them, too. They heard the roar of animals, the crash of thunder, the rush of a river. And people started to imitate the sounds around them with sounds of their own. They clapped their hands and stamped their feet or used sticks and stones to make distinct noises.

This was how instruments that you hit, shake, or scrape came to be. We call them percussion instruments. Gradually, these early instruments became more complicated. Banging a piece of wood made one sound. If the wood was hollowed out, the sound improved. And if a piece of animal skin was stretched over the hollowed wood, the sound was even better. Drums like this dating from prehistoric times have been discovered.

Noise from vibrations

A drum is a very simple instrument. It can be made by tightly stretching a thin skin, or membrane, over a simple frame. The beat sound arises when you tap on the skin with your fingers or hands, like the drummer in the picture. Or you can use a beater. The drummer in the second picture is using two sticks to beat his drums. This makes the skin shake, or vibrate, with tiny movements, and as the skin vibrates, so does the air around it. We call these air vibrations sound waves.

A drummer from Ghana

When the sound waves spread down into the hollow part of the drum, they echo around and grow louder. When sound waves act like this, we call it resonating.

Make a drum

You can easily make your own drum. Find a mixing bowl or a tin. Stretch waxed paper or cloth tightly over the top. Fasten it over the rim with string or a rubber band. Or you can use lengths of overlapping tape to make the membrane. Tap the top of the drum gently with a pencil or a spoon. If you scatter a few grains of salt on the membrane, you'll be able to see how the vibration causes the salt to bounce.

Can you hear the note the drum makes? Press lightly on one edge of the paper and tap it again. Is the note higher this time? It should be! That's because you have made the membrane tighter. The tightness of a membrane is known as its tension.

How do you hear sounds?

Did you realize you have two drums inside your head? They are your eardrums! Each eardrum is a membrane that works in much the same way as the drum that you hit. Your outer ear acts like a funnel collecting sound waves from the air around you. The sound travels down a tube called the ear canal until it hits your eardrum. The sound waves make the eardrum vibrate. The vibrations travel inward to some tiny bones in the inner ear.

Now the vibrations are twenty times stronger. They are passed to the cochlea, which contains three tubes coiled like a snail's shell. The tubes are full of liquid.

When vibrations reach the cochlea, they make the liquid move. This moves hairs in one of the coils, which in turn causes nerve endings to send messages to the brain. These tell you all about the sound you've heard. The way we hear sounds is a complicated process – and we are not even aware that it's happening.

How loud is loud?

The loudness of a sound is measured on a scale of units called decibels. Very loud sounds, such as explosions, have the highest decibel reading. They can burst your eardrum, so people who work with noisy machinery wear ear protectors.

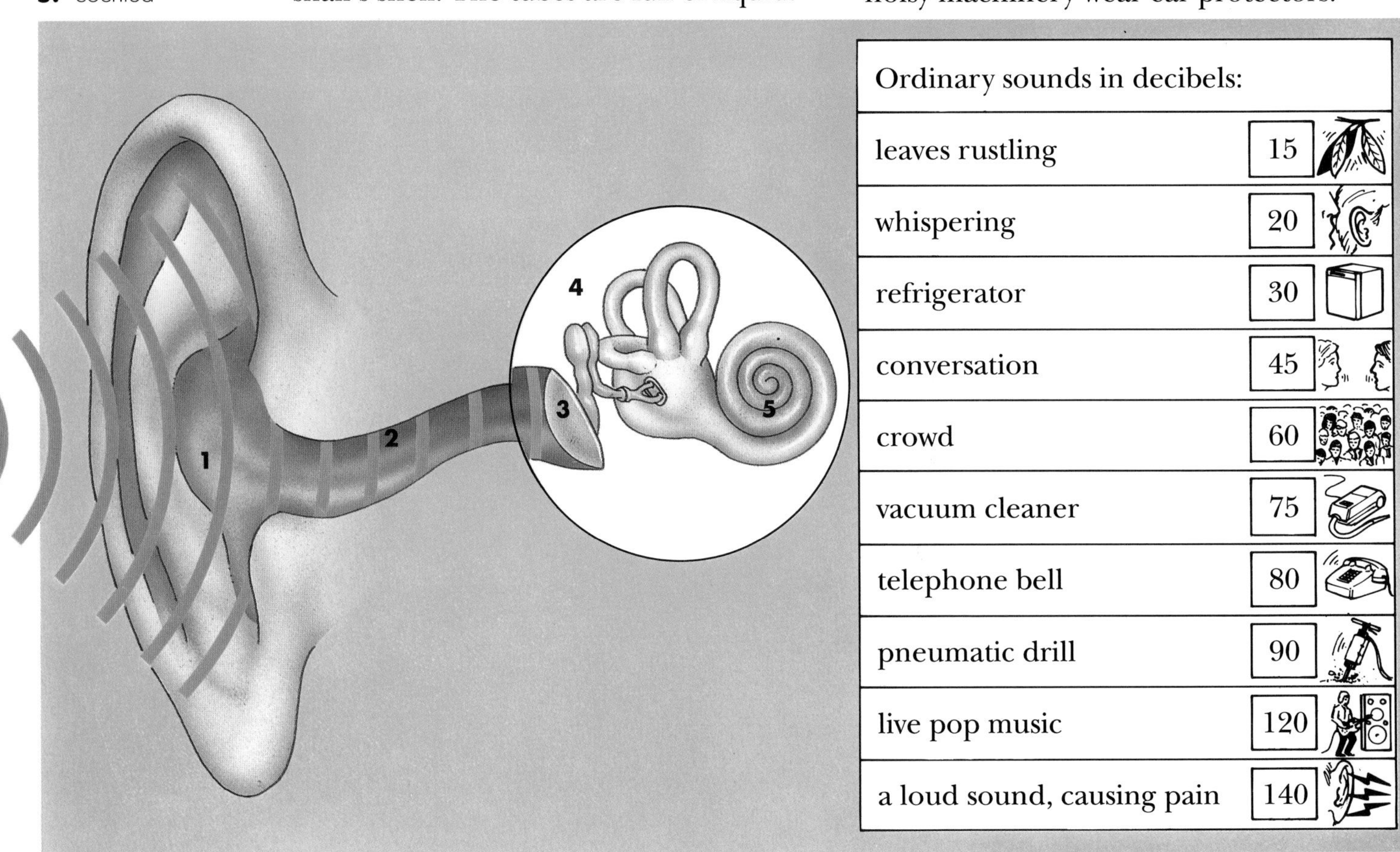

A diagram of the ear, showing:

1. outer ear
2. ear canal
3. eardrum
4. bones
5. cochlea

Ordinary sounds in decibels:	
leaves rustling	15
whispering	20
refrigerator	30
conversation	45
crowd	60
vacuum cleaner	75
telephone bell	80
pneumatic drill	90
live pop music	120
a loud sound, causing pain	140

The German composer Ludwig van Beethoven

Hearing difficulties

In the past, people with poor hearing used a large funnel called an ear trumpet to help them hear better. When they held it to their ear, the trumpet shape acted like a large second ear, collecting more sound. The great German composer Ludwig van Beethoven used an ear trumpet when he was becoming deaf. Today, technology provides electronic hearing aids, which are much more efficient than ear trumpets. And even people who can't hear can play musical instruments. This picture shows the Scottish percussionist Evelyn Glennie. Despite being deaf, she is one of the most skilful percussionists in the world today.

The Scottish percussionist Evelyn Glennie

Different kinds of drums

Drums are made all over the world, and traditionally they have been made from whatever materials were on hand. Drums are often made of wood, but can also be made of clay or metal. In Arctic regions there are no trees, so the Eskimo people, the Inuits, might use bone as a frame for a drum. The membrane is usually made of animal skin. Of course, the type of skin also depends on what is available. Drum membranes have been made from snakeskin and even from elephants' ears.

Adding paste

Some Indian and African drum makers rub a circular patch of paste onto the membrane of their drum. In Africa, the paste is usually made from a mixture of beeswax and roasted peanut powder. In India they use rice and ashes. When the player beats on the special patch, the sound produced is lower than in other places on the membrane.

Pastes made from rice, peanut powder, beeswax and ashes

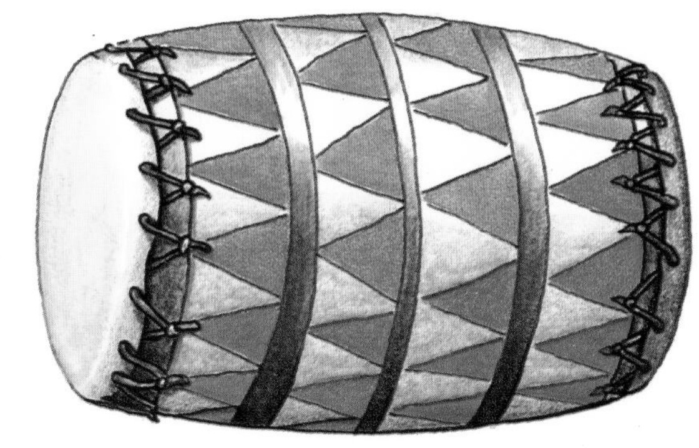

1

Thin and fat

Drums come in many different shapes and sizes. The pictures above show you the six main shapes. The barrel drum has a membrane at each end, so it is played on its side. Some barrel drums have only one membrane and can be stood on end to be played. Waisted drums have a pinched-in waist. They can also have one or two membranes. Goblet drums are shaped like drinking cups or glasses. They have a wide membrane at the top and a narrow foot to support them on the ground.

Long drums are tall and thin, with a single membrane. Frame drums have one membrane stretched over a shallow frame, which is usually round. Finally, there are vessel drums which are bowl-shaped drums with a single membrane. These are also called kettledrums because kettle is an old word for a cooking pot.

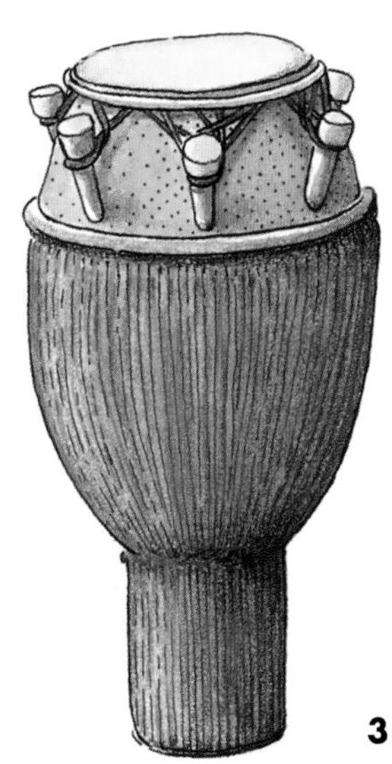

1. A barrel drum from Nigeria
2. A waisted drum from Japan
3. A goblet drum from Ghana
4. A long drum from New Guinea
5. A North American Indian frame drum
6. A kettledrum from India

Making a noise

Drums are often used to accompany dancing, as in this picture showing Chinese dancers. They are also used in religious ceremonies, for sending messages, for frightening an enemy or as a way of praying for good weather. In Europe in the 1500s, they were even used by dentists. While a patient was having a tooth pulled out, a drum was beaten to drown out the yells!

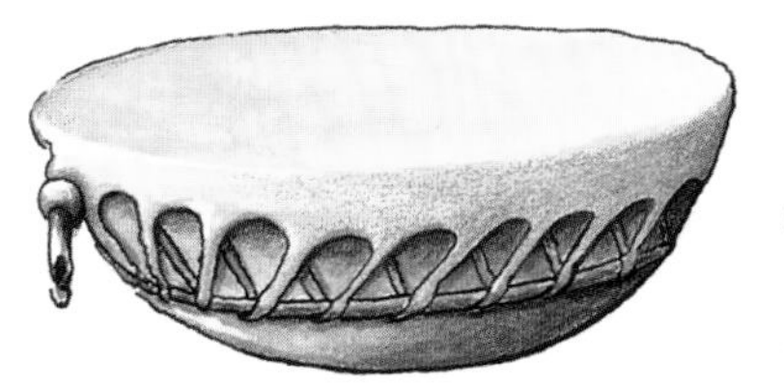

Dancing drummers from China

Sounding a drum

This drummer is part of an Indian picture called *Three Musicians and a Dancing Girl*

To make a drum sound, you have to make the drum's membrane vibrate by hitting it. You already know that you can strike a drum with your fingers or hands or use drum sticks or beaters. Small drums such as the Indian one in this picture are usually played with the fingers or hands. The larger drums, such as the bass drum, are usually played with beaters. Look at the sticks and beaters in the picture below. You will see that some have padded ends. Can you see the wire brush? This makes a swishing sound when it hits the membrane.

The type of drum-hitter you use makes all the difference to the sound your drum makes. If you hit a drum with a stick, it makes a hard, clear sound. If you hit it with a padded beater, it sounds softer and muffled. Try hitting a homemade drum with any stick-shaped thing you can find – a wooden spoon, a hairbrush or a bunch of twigs. They will all produce interesting noises from your drum.

Wire brushes and felt-headed beaters

Beater heads

The padding on the heads of beaters can be made from felt, leather, wood, cork, rubber or plastic. You could use other materials to make your own beaters.

You will need some thin sticks, about 20 centimetres long, and anything you can think of to make a soft head. Look at this picture for some ideas. To make a soft beater, cut a round piece of cloth and fill it with cotton wool. Wrap it round the stick and tie it on. For a harder beater, you could trim the sides of a large cork to make it round, or you could try fixing a small rubber ball to the end of a stick. Or you could wrap lots of rubber bands around the stick until you have a rounded shape.

Now you can experiment with the different beaters. But be careful when you beat your homemade drum. If you hit the membrane too hard, you might make a hole in it.

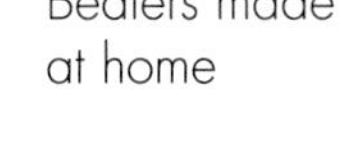

Beaters made at home

Rhythm and pulse

You know that drums produce a strong, repetitive pattern of sound called a rhythm. If you march along like the girl above, your feet make a rhythm. You can write this marching rhythm down as music. You have to use a mark to represent each distinct footstep. These marks are called notes and when the notes making up your rhythm are written, they look like this:

You'll see there are two notes in every section, or bar. We call these notes pulses, or beats. The pulse is the heartbeat of music. A doctor has to feel your pulse to find out how regularly your heart is beating, but you can hear the beat in music just by listening!

Most western music is made up of regular patterns of beats. It is these patterns of beats which make up the rhythm of a piece of music. Modern composers arrange groups of beats in many different ways to make interesting rhythms. If you listen to a piece of music called *The Rite of Spring*, by the Russian composer Igor Stravinsky, you will hear some very unusual and exciting rhythms.

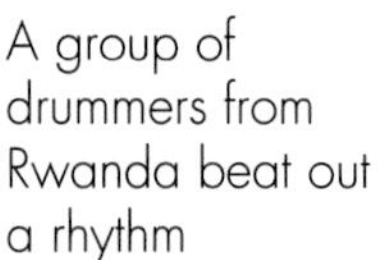

A group of drummers from Rwanda beat out a rhythm

Marching beat

Accents and rest

Most western music has a rhythm of two or three beats. But how can we tell when the beats fall, when each one is followed by thousands of other notes which make up the piece of music? The answer is that certain notes in the group are more strongly stressed than others. They are accented.

The next time you listen to some music, see if you can tell where the accented notes are. Listen to marches that follow a **one**-two, **one**-two beat, or rock songs which stress the first of four beats – **one**, two, three, four. If you listen carefully, you will be able to count how many beats there are in each bar.

Composers sometimes change the normal pulse by putting accents on beats that you would expect to be unaccented. This is called syncopation. You will often hear syncopated rhythms in jazz. Sometimes there's a gap, or rest, in the music, when the instrument does not play. These rests also make up part of the rhythmical pattern.

African rhythms

You can hear some exciting rhythms in African music. In some musical groups, there may be as many as twelve musicians, all playing different rhythms at the same time. Each player follows a set pattern of rhythm which fits into the patterns played by the rest of the drummers.

Rhythms in eastern music

Much of the music of India and other parts of Asia does not follow the same regular rhythm patterns as western music. Eastern music is often not written down. Instead, it is made up by the musicians as they play, using complicated rules of rhythm. You can read more about drumming in India on pages 22 and 23.

Talking drums

A talking drummer from Nigeria

In some languages of the world, the same word can be spoken in two ways to give two quite different meanings. If you say the word in a high tone, it means something completely different from the same word spoken in a low tone.

One such language is Yoruba, spoken by the people of northern Nigeria. These people use drums to send messages in Yoruba. They use a large drum for the low tones and a small one for the high tones. In this way, a drummer can send messages to people up to 30 kilometres away. Some Nigerian drummers are so skillful that they can send messages using only one drum, like the one in the picture. But how do they vary the tones so that their drums 'talk'?

You can change the tone of a drum by changing the tension of the membrane. A tighter membrane gives a higher tone. The membrane can be firmly attached to the body of the drum by gluing, nailing or lacing. Lacing is done in different patterns, as you can see in the pictures below.

Different patterns of lacing:

1. N lacing
2. W lacing
3. X lacing
4. Y lacing
5. Net lacing

1
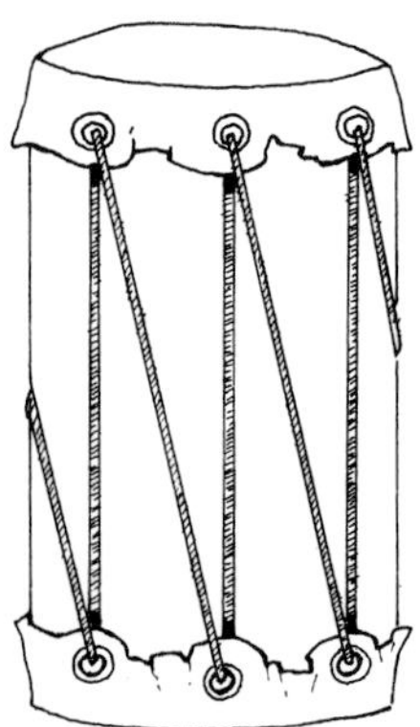

2
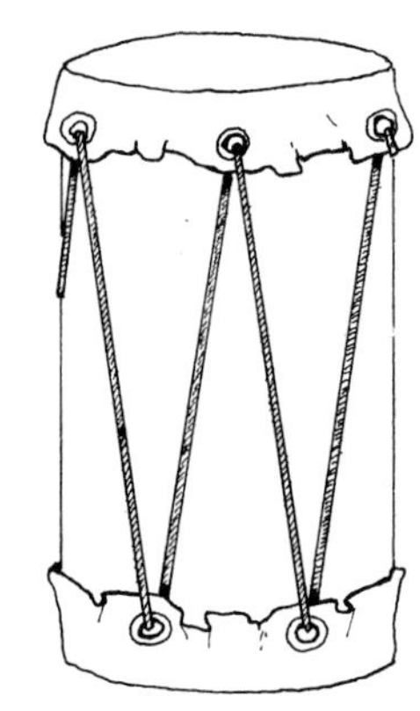

3
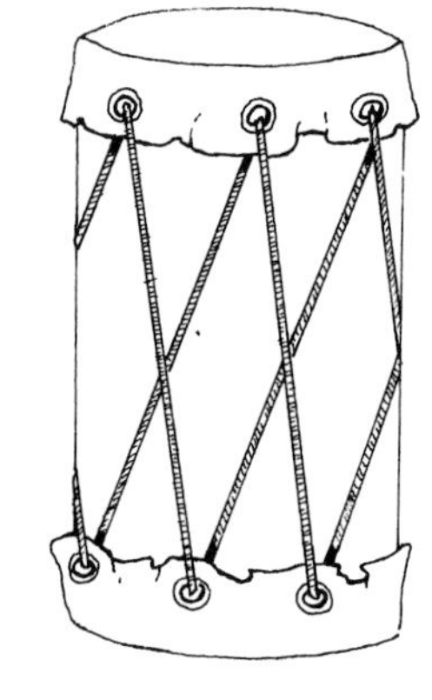

4
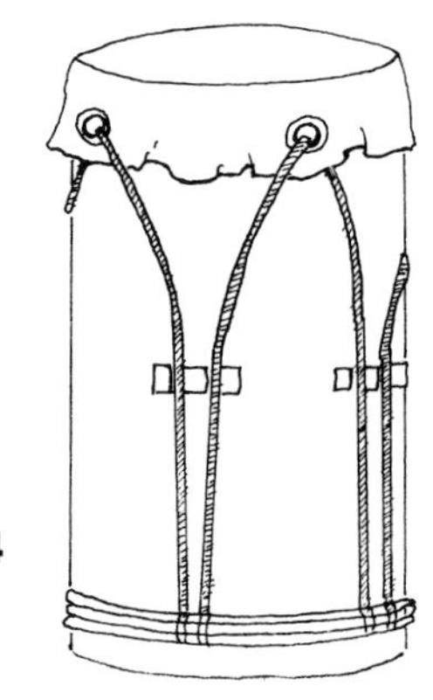

5
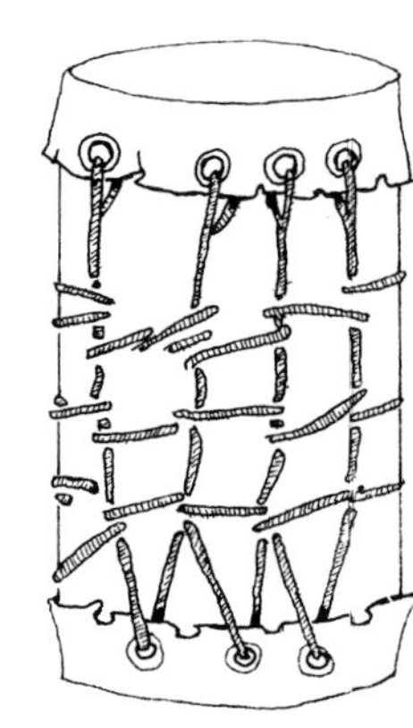

A Nigerian talking drum

N-shaped lacing

The talking drum of Nigeria is laced very simply. The picture above shows you the tight N-shaped lacing in detail. As the drummer strikes the drum, using a crooked L-shaped beater, he adjusts the tightness of the lacing with the other hand. He pulls the membrane tighter to give a higher tone, or relaxes it to make the tone lower.

Tapping out words

You can use a beater and your homemade drum to tap out the rhythm of people's names. Even when two words have the same number of syllables, their rhythmic patterns can be quite different. Try tapping 'tambourine' and then 'Africa'. You will hear that the rhythms are different. Some speech rhythms are fun to copy. Or try your favourite rhyme. But beware! English is not a tone language, like Yoruba, so 'shut the door' will sound the same as 'spill the beans'.

A drum on a frame

The Irish folk group The Chieftains

Old Irish tales say that there was once only one drum in all of Ireland. It was shared by two friends. One day, they both needed the drum at the same time and could not agree on who should have it. They asked the advice of a wise man, who told them to cut the drum in two. The friends each went away with half the drum. And that, so the story says, is why the Irish drum, called the bodhran, has only one skin! The bodhran, pronounced 'bawren', is the favourite drum in Irish folk music. You can see one being played by a member of the Irish folk band The Chieftains in the picture.

Gentle or exciting

The bodhran can accompany a sad love song, beat a rousing march and urge on the energetic Irish dance called the reel. The sound of a bodhran depends on how it's made. The membrane was traditionally made of goatskin and the frame of ash wood.

A pin

A flick of the wrist

Playing the bodhran requires great skill. You hold the sticks at the back of the drum with your left hand. In your right hand, you hold the double-headed drumstick, called a pin. Look at the picture above to see what a pin looks like. You hold it like a pencil and flick your wrist backwards and forwards hitting the skin with both ends of the pin.

A drummer from Siberia

Magical powers

Another type of drum is played by people in northern Russia and by North American Indians. It is usually round, like the Siberian drum in the picture. An animal skin is stretched over the frame and the player holds the lacing like a handle. This kind of drum was mainly used to accompany sacred songs and rituals. It was also used to help communicate with the spirits of dead people or to pray for good weather. It was even thought to have magical powers in the hands of a medicine man.

Friction drums

An engraving of a rommelpot player by the Dutch artist Frans Hals

Friction is another way of saying rubbing. If you lick your finger and rub it over a tight drum membrane, it makes a grinding noise. Most friction drums have a hole in the drum membrane and a stick pushed into the hole makes a dramatic growling sound when it is rubbed round and round or up and down. The stick makes the whole drum vibrate.

Rommelpots

Rommelpots were popular friction drums in Europe. This picture of a rommelpot player is by the Dutch artist Frans Hals. Children used to make them out of a kitchen pot which they covered with an animal skin. They sometimes used mustard jars or even thimbles. Then they pierced the skin with a wet stick and rubbed the stick up and down. These rommelpots were often played at celebrations and religious festivals.

A friction drum from Zambia

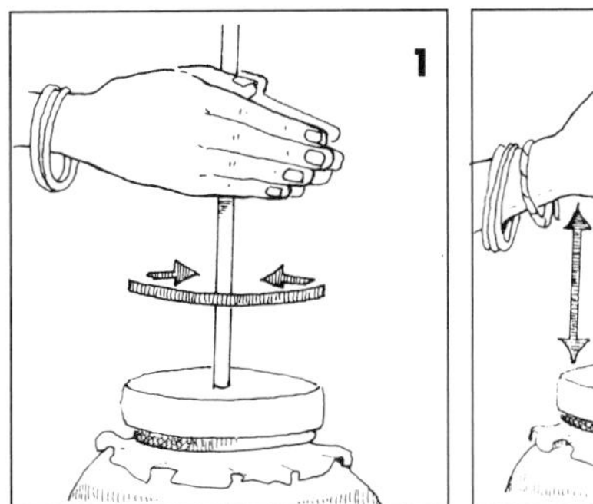

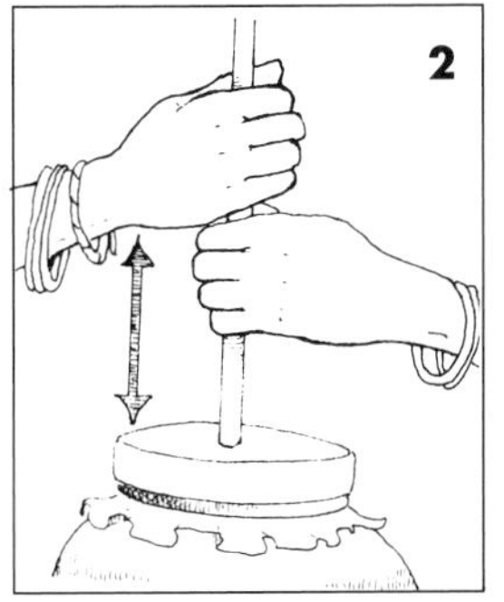

1. Rubbing the stick between the hands to turn it
2. Pulling the stick up and down

The lion roar

Friction drums like the one in the picture below are sometimes used in bands and orchestras. These drums have a string passed through the drumhead instead of a stick. The string is rubbed with the same soft sticky gum called resin that is used for violin bows. When you slide a piece of soft leather up the string, you get a gravelly, growling noise. This noise gives the drum its name.

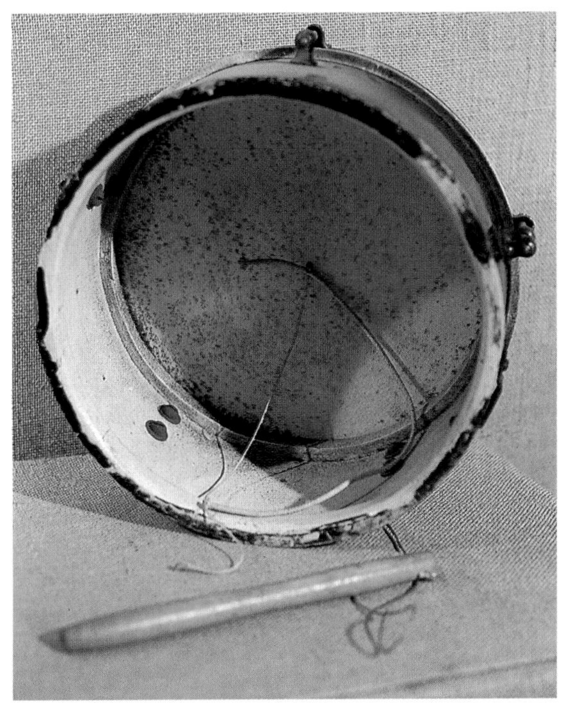

An English lion roar

Moving the stick

The beautiful friction drum in the picture above is from Zambia. You can see the stick piercing its membrane. The diagrams at the top of the page show you how the stick is moved to make a sound. It can be pulled up and down or turned by rubbing it between the hands.

Mirlitons and pellet drums

If you wrap a piece of tissue paper round a comb, put your lips on the paper and hum or sing, your voice will be disguised. It will make a strange buzzing sound! This happens because the air coming out of your mouth makes the tissue paper membrane vibrate. You feel the vibrations tickling your lips as you blow.

Your tissue paper and comb are creating a mirliton. A mirliton is not so much a musical instrument as a gadget for changing the sound of a musical note.

Mirlitons can also be made from a cow's horn or from a dried hollow vegetable called a gourd. A thin membrane made from the web-like material which spiders spin to protect their eggs, or from parts of a bat's wing, provides the buzzing sound.

Two or three hundred years ago, European eunuch flutes worked in the same way. These instruments were also known as onion flutes, because onion skins were sometimes used as membranes. The player spoke or sang into the membrane over the hole at the end of the instrument.

A French eunuch flute

A kazoo is a toy mirliton with a tissue paper membrane located half-way down its length. You can see the circle of paper at the side of the picture. When you sing or talk into the tube, the paper vibrates to make your voice sound different, just like the tissue paper around your comb.

A modern kazoo

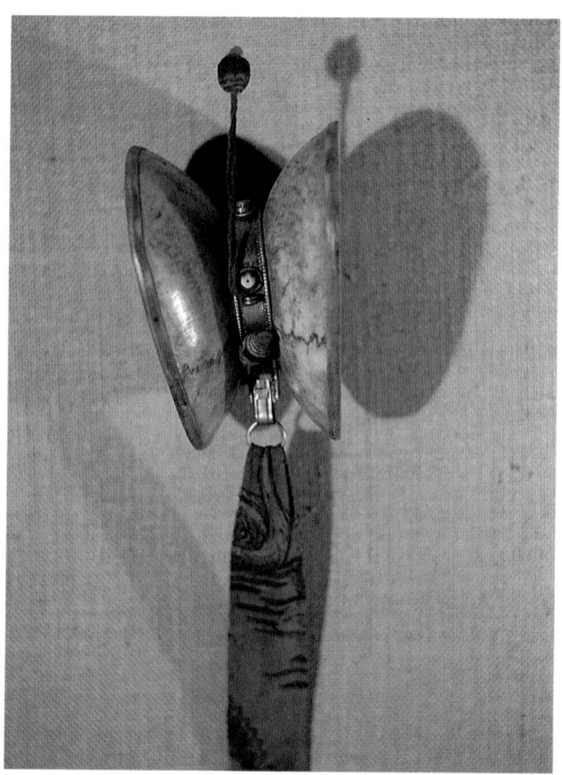

A pellet drum
from Tibet

Pellet drum

Drums like the Tibetan drum in the picture above are unusual because they are not played with hands or sticks. They are played with beads or pellets. Two frames are joined together, with each open end covered with a membrane. A string with pellets attached is tied around the middle.

When the drum is shaken, the pellets hit against the membrane, first at one end and then at the other. The Tibetan drum is gruesome as well as unusual. It is made from two human skulls which have been cut in half! Each half is covered by a membrane. These are hit by the bead on the string.

Make a yoghurt pot drum

Cover the open ends of two yoghurt pots with some waxed paper and attach it tightly with string or rubber bands. Then glue the pots together, with the paper-covered ends facing outwards. Thread some beads onto string, making sure that the string is the right length to hit the paper at each end of the drum. Tie the string around the middle and your drum is ready to play.

Indian drums

Playing the tabla

Pairs of drums

The tabla are the drums you see being used most often by small groups of musicians in India. Tabla is the name for a pair of drums. The larger drum, called the bhaya, has a metal body. The smaller one, the tabla, has a wooden body. The tabla is always positioned on the drummer's right-hand side and the bhaya on the left.

The tabla

Indian drummers are said to be the best in the world. They can hear the difference between 15 and 16 very fast beats in a bar. Ask a friend to beat on the table 15 times and then again 16 times. Can you hear the difference? A drummer needs years and years of learning and practice to become so skilled in hearing rhythm.

A tabla from southern India

One hand or two

The drummer must learn to play each drum on its own and both drums at the same time. And the tabla can be played with one hand or with both hands together! Drummers usually squat on the ground and cradle the drums in their lap to play them. Each drum has a different tone, one higher than the other.

The sound each drum makes can be changed by spreading paste over the membrane. Small blocks of wood can also be placed under the lacing of the tabla to tighten the membrane and make the tone higher.

The bhaya

Finding the rhythm

Tabla players often play in a group, with musicians playing two stringed instruments called the sitar and the tambura. The music is not written down but is made up as the players go along. The drums play in a rhythm called a tala. A tala is a regular beat which the player uses throughout the piece of music. There can be anything from 3 to 100 beats in every bar and rhythms of 5, 7, 11 or 14 beats in a bar are quite usual. A special rhythm, called the Savari rhythm, has 11 beats in a bar, divided into sections of 4, 4, 1½ and 1½ beats. If you turn back to pages 12 and 13 to see that most western music has two or three beats in a bar, you will see how complicated the tala rhythm is.

Music in the world of Islam

It seems quite natural for us to have music whenever we want it. We can sing, we can play an instrument, we can listen to a tape. But it has not always been like this everywhere in the world. The prophet Mohammed, who founded the Islamic religion, did not approve of musical instruments. In the early days, singing was allowed, but only for religious purposes. A singer could chant from The Koran and call people to the mosque to pray. This is why Islamic music may have started as a single tune without any extra notes. People made up the music as they sang or drummed.

As time went by, people performed more kinds of music and introduced more kinds of instruments.

A pair of darbukas

Using drums

Arab people played many different musical instruments. You can see a band of Arabic musicians playing lively music on various instruments at the top of the page. Drums were especially popular. They were used in marriage celebrations and great religious festivals. Military processions were accompanied by drumming.

The darbuka

So what were Arabic drums like? Frame drums, like the one in the top picture, were popular, and kettledrums were used for military processions. But the most beautiful drum to look at was a goblet drum called the darbuka.

A painting of Arabic musicians from the 1800s

A painted darbuka from the Middle East

The darbuka is a goblet-shaped drum made from pottery or wood. You can see that the darbuka was beautifully painted and some were decorated with mosaic patterns of gleaming tortoiseshell and mother-of-pearl.

Darbuka are small drums, so they are easy to carry. Players in Iraq tuck them under their arm and hit them from the side with flat hands. The player can stand up or sit down like the drummer in the picture on the right. Sometimes the hitting surface is raised above the rim of the drum to make it easier to play.

Playing the darbuka

Drums for dancing

Music and dance played an important part in the lives of North American Apache Indians. Look at the picture below. The Apaches are dancing at a celebration. They circle the campfire, linking arms in a line as a singer sings in a high nasal voice. The dancers move four steps forwards and then back again. Gradually, the whole circle moves clockwise round the fire in a steady rhythm. The water drum played by the crouching drummer in the foreground provides this rhythm.

Loosened by water

American Indian water drums were made from an iron kettle, with a membrane of tanned buckskin. The drum was one-third full of water. As the drum was played, water splashed against the skin. This loosened the skin to make an interesting sound. The drummer beat the skin with a thin drumstick which had a loop at the end. The soft booming noise was quite unlike the sound of any other type of drum.

An Apache social dance

Samba dancers at the carnival in Rio de Janeiro, Brazil

Latin American rhythms

Ask anyone what makes Latin American music different from other music and you'll probably get one answer – rhythm. Drummers beat out the rhythms with such energy and enthusiasm that it's impossible not to get up and dance.Have you heard of the rumba, or the samba, or the bossa nova? These are all Latin American dances with special rhythms. Perhaps you can do one of them!

Latin American dance bands usually have more than one drum. The smallest ones are the bongos. Bongos are a pair of small drums which are open at the bottom. One drum is a little bigger than the other, so they play different notes. The drums are held between the knees and played with the fingers and hands, making a high, dry, tapping noise.

Timbales are similar to the bongos, but larger. Barrel-shaped congas are the largest drums in the band.

There are usually two or three congas in each dance band. They can be played with a cupped hand as well as with the fingers and they make a full, deep sound that drives the beat of this dance music.

Look at the picture of women dancing the samba at the carnival in Rio de Janeiro. This carnival takes place every year. People compete for prizes awarded for the best costumes and the best dancers.

A pair of bongos

Drums from Japan

Listen to some traditional Japanese music. You will notice that each instrument or voice follows the same main tune, called the melody. Drums play an especially important part in supporting the melody. They provide a background of strong beats to keep the melody moving along to the right rhythm.

Gagaku

Gagaku is the official music played in the Japanese imperial court. It is one of the oldest forms of Japanese music.

There are two kinds of drum and one gong in the group of instruments, or ensemble, that plays gagaku music. The largest instrument, the tsuri-daiko, hangs from a decorated wooden stand. You can see a tsuri-daiko in the picture below. It is played with two sticks.

A gagaku ensemble

The kakko rests on a low stand. The player hits both heads of the drum. The kakko is often used to play interesting rhythms. It has two membranes, one at each end, which are both beaten. The third instrument in the picture above is a gong.

A da-daiko from Japan

Japanese theatre

A Japanese drum called the ko-tsuzumi is very important to the music of Japanese theatre. This drum is an hourglass shape and is painted black with gold decoration. It has two membranes made of horsehide stretched over iron rings. Small patches of paper are put on one of the membranes to make the sound more interesting. The two heads are bound together by a long cord which the player squeezes to make the skin tighter and so produce a higher note. The drum is held against the player's right shoulder. You can tell how skilled the drummer is by the colour of the cord on his drum. Orange-red cord is used by ordinary players, light blue by more advanced players and lilac by masters of the art.

There is also a huge drum called a da-daiko which is used on special occasions. It is set on a special platform, in an elaborately decorated frame, with steps leading up to it. As you can see in the picture above, the drummer puts his left foot on the platform and his right foot on the upper step.

The ko-tsuzumi provides a rhythmic accompaniment to the drama, called 'No' theatre. In 'No' theatre, the actors wear masks and chant words to the accompaniment of music played by musicians on stage. A chorus of singers describes what is happening and comments on it.

A scene from a Japanese 'No' drama

From kettledrums to timpani

A pair of naqara

A kettledrum was originally just a membrane stretched over a cooking pot – a very simple instrument. Then, gradually, people started making vessels especially for drums.

Kettledrums today are often played in pairs, with each drum sounding a different note. The Arab naqara are a pair of small kettledrums with wood or clay bodies. The membrane is laced onto the drum and beaten with small sticks. The membrane can be tightened by twisting a stick through the lacing to produce a higher note.

Nakers

Soldiers from Europe, called crusaders, went to the Middle East to fight in wars during in the 1100s and 1200s. There they heard the exciting sound of the Arab naqara, which were played by the enemy as a sign for the battle to begin. They were very impressed by the sound and many soldiers brought naqara back to Europe. In England, they were called nakers and came to be used in military battles, in dance music and in church processions.

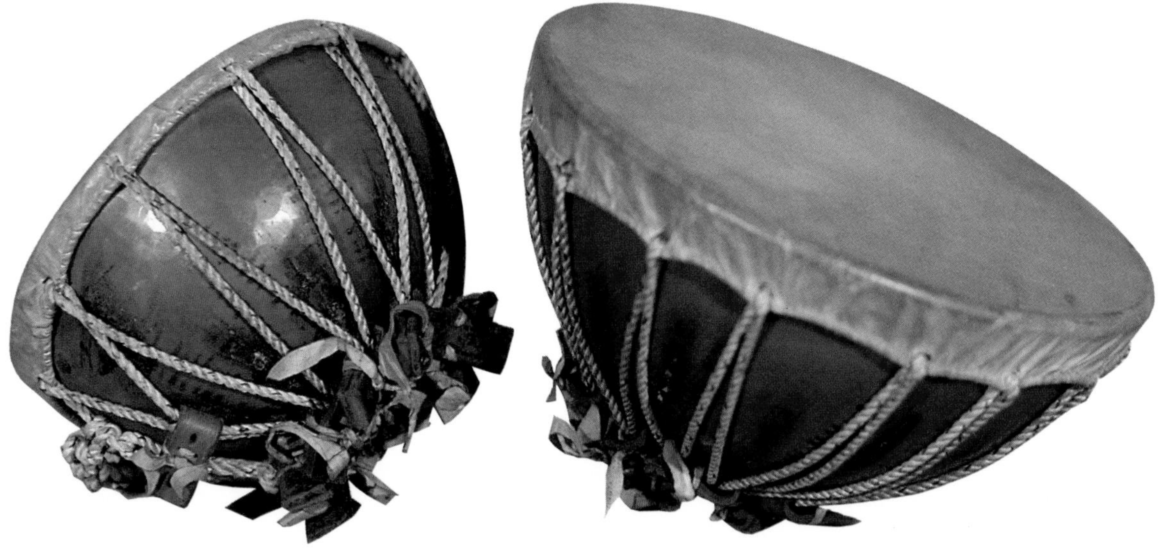

European nakers from the 1200s

Carried on horseback

Years ago, large kettledrums were played on horseback, or even on the back of a camel in Egypt and Arabia. A drum was suspended on each side of the player. A trumpet was often played at the same time. Kettledrums were sometimes even mounted on a carriage and taken into battle.

Tuning a kettledrum

Kettledrums can be tuned to change their note to a higher or lower sound. This is called changing the pitch of a note. To make them easy to tune accurately, a hoop was fixed round the top of the drum, with screws set round it. The screws could be tightened or loosened to change the tension of the membrane. Turning the screws to tune the drums in the middle of a performance is difficult.

Timpani

Modern orchestral kettledrums are known as timpani. The bowls are usually made from fibreglass and the membranes from plastic. Timpani are much easier to tune. Many have a pedal that adjusts the tension of the membrane. Others have a handle at the top of the drum to do the same job. A range of sticks is used to play timpani, but perhaps the most common are felt-headed beaters like the ones in the picture below.

Kettledrums used in the Trooping the Colour ceremony in London

Timpani beaters

Orchestral drums

If you listen to *Peter and the Wolf* by the Russian composer Sergei Prokofiev you will hear the orchestral timpani and bass drum used very effectively. They mimic the sound of hunters shooting their guns in the forest. It is very realistic!

In a western orchestra, the drums are part of the percussion section, which is right at the back in the centre.

Playing orchestral timpani

A bass drum

In a large orchestra, you'll probably see a bass drum and a side drum. A side drum is a small drum fitted with snares, which you can read about on pages 34 and 35. You will also see between two and four kettledrums, called timpani. You can find out more about timpani on pages 30 and 31.

There may also be a tambourine, which you can read more about on pages 38 and 39, and a gong drum. The French composer Hector Berlioz asks for 16 kettledrums to be played by 10 drummers in one of his works!

The bass drum

The bass drum is the largest orchestral drum. It is so heavy that it is hung in a frame and can be hit from either side. The bass drummer uses many different beaters to give different effects. Its deep, booming stroke makes an unearthly sound. The biggest bass drum ever made measured about 4 metres across, but most bass drums are more likely to be about 1.3 metres across.

There is some interesting music for the orchestra's percussion section to play. Drums are no longer just for giving the beat. They've become musical instruments in their own right. The British composer Benjamin Britten wrote *The Young Person's Guide to the Orchestra*, in which the percussion instruments show just what they can do!

A bass drum beater

The snare drum

A soldier marching with a snare drum

Look at the drum this soldier is playing as he marches along. It is called a snare drum. Snare drums are sometimes called side drums, because of the way soldiers carry them on their left side. They are made of wood or metal, with a plastic or calfskin membrane on both sides of the frame. There are eight or more strands of wire or nylon stretched tightly over the lower membrane.

These wire strands are called snares. When the drum is hit, the snares vibrate with the skin. This makes a biting, cracking sound. To stop the snares from vibrating, the drummer presses a lever at the side of the drum and this loosens the snares. Sometimes, drummers tuck a piece of cloth between the snares and the head to make sure there is no vibration.

A modern snare drum

1

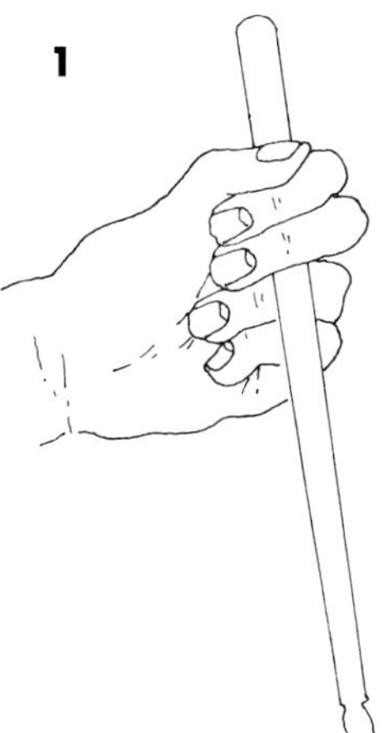

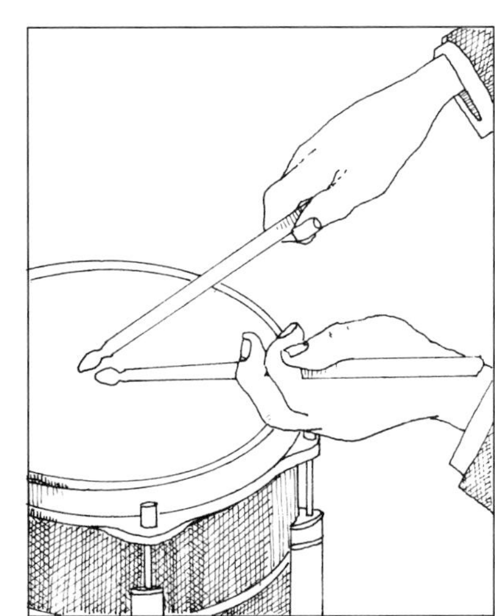

2

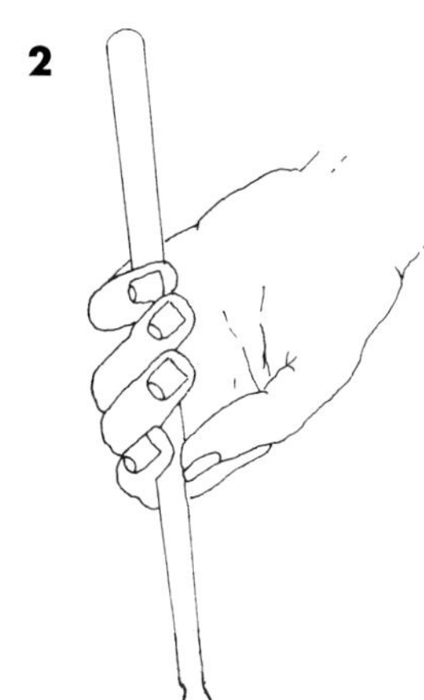

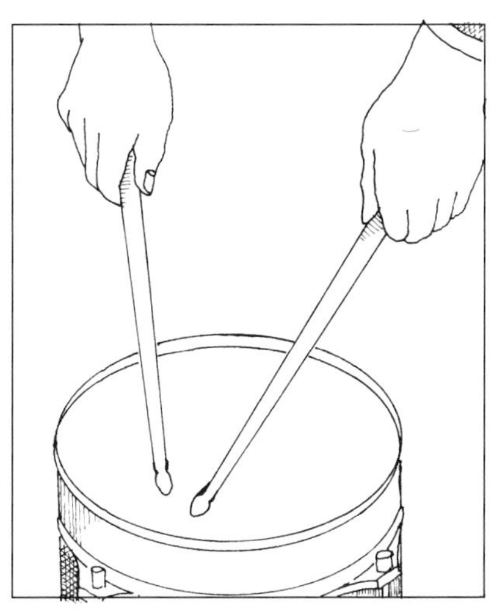

1. The rabbit grip
2. The matched grip

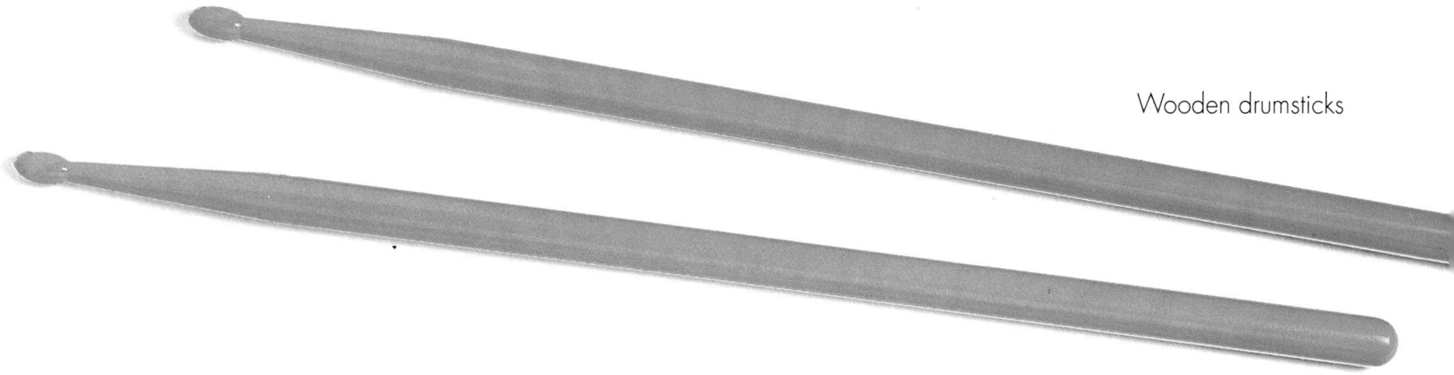

Roll your drum

So how do you play a snare drum as you march along on parade? First, you have to choose the right sticks. Heavy wooden sticks with large tips like the ones in the picture are best. They make a hard, strong sound as they hit the drum.

Now you must learn to hold the sticks correctly. There are different ways of doing this. The first picture above shows the traditional grip. This is the best grip to use when you're marching. You hold the stick between the two middle fingers. This is sometimes called the rabbit grip. Do you think it has the shape of a rabbit?

The second picture shows a different grip called the matched grip. This grip is useful to learn because many other drums are played like this. You hold the stick in your fist.

Then comes the playing. Drummers have to make sure they strike the centre of the drum with crisp, even strokes. But you can practise beating on any surface. Start with left stick (L) and right stick (R) taking it in turns – L R L R L R. Can you hear the rhythm? Lots of rhythms have names to help you get them right. You could do the 'Mummy/Daddy' roll, which goes like this: L L R R L L R R L L R R. Try it – it's not as difficult as you think!

Wooden drumsticks

The march of military bands

This picture, called *Music at the Customs House at Le Havre*, was painted by the French artist Raoul Dufy

You've already looked at the snare drum, which soldiers play on parade. But marching bands play lots of other drums, too. There's nothing like a good steady beat from a big bass drum to keep everyone in step. Military bands have kept weary soldiers marching to a regular beat for many years. They are exciting to watch, too. Perhaps you have stood and cheered while a large, colourful band like the one in the picture above marched by.

Drum and fife bands consist of fifes, which are small flutes, side drums, bass drum, cymbals and triangles. The shrill noise of the fifes dancing over the top of the beating percussion makes an exciting sound. Bigger military bands also contain brass instruments. The players' music is clipped onto small music holders called lyres. These are attached to the instruments so that the players can read the music as they march along.

Felt-headed bass drum beaters

The March King

The best-known composer of military marches is the American composer John Philip Sousa. He composed over one hundred marches and came to be known as the March King. Sousa played in the United States Marine band for five years and later became its bandmaster. Then in 1892, he started his own band, Sousa's Band.

John Philip Sousa

Carrying a bass drum

Look at the bass drum in the picture on the right of this page. Bass drums made for marching can be more than 70 centimetres across so, as you can imagine, marching along with one strapped to your chest is not easy.

You need long arms to hit the membranes on both sides with the felt-headed beaters, too! The bass drum is the instrument that sets the pace of the marching. Brisk marching speed is about 112 paces to the minute. You could time yourself to see if this is a comfortable speed. How many paces do you march in one minute?

A bass drum for marching

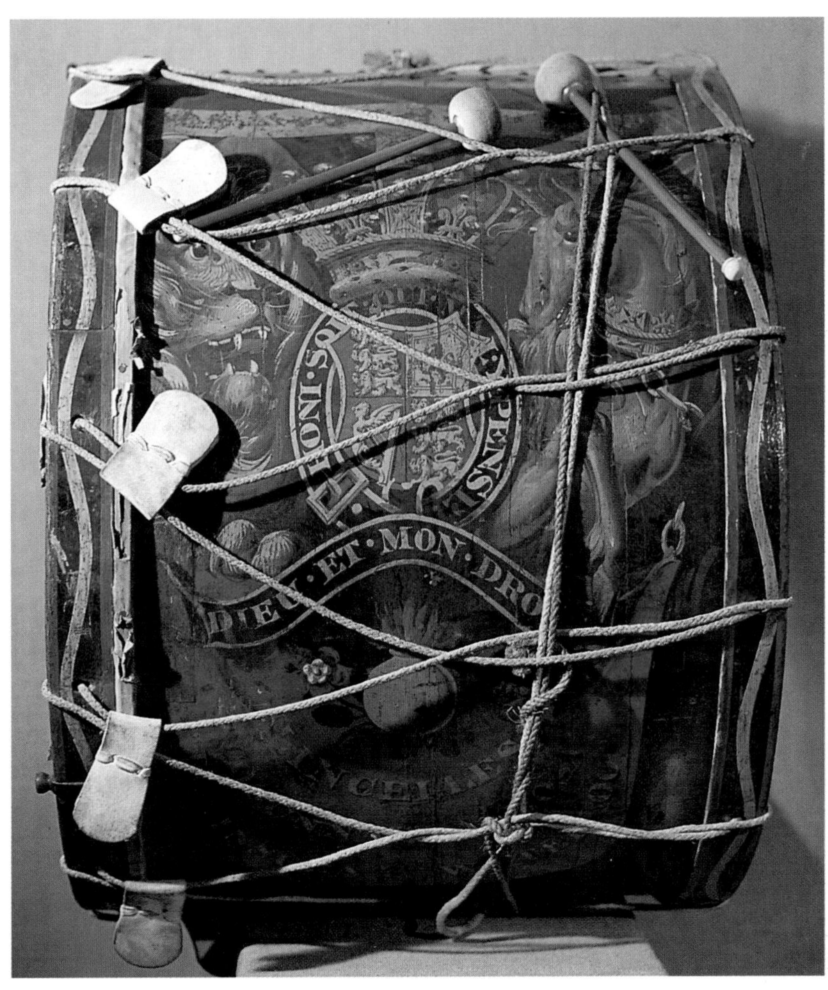

Beating the tambourine

'And Miriam the prophetess, the sister of Aaron, took a timbrel in her hand; and all the women went out after her with timbrels and dances'.

This is just one of many mentions of the timbrel, or tambourine, in The Bible. The tambourine is a very ancient instrument. Just like a simple drum, it has a frame with a single membrane stretched across it. But a tambourine often has metal discs attached to its frame. So a tambourine can be hit like a drum or shaken like a rattle.

Different tambourines

The pictures below show three different kinds of tambourine. The first is called a bendir and comes from Morocco. Can you see two strings stretched across it? These are snares, which work just like the snares on a snare drum. The second tambourine comes from Japan and the third from England.

Modern tambourines

Modern tambourines are a round wooden hoop with a plastic skin nailed or glued to one side. Most modern tambourines have pairs of metal jingle plates fixed around the edge.

1. A Moroccan bendir
2. A Japanese tambourine
3. A British tambourine from the 1800s

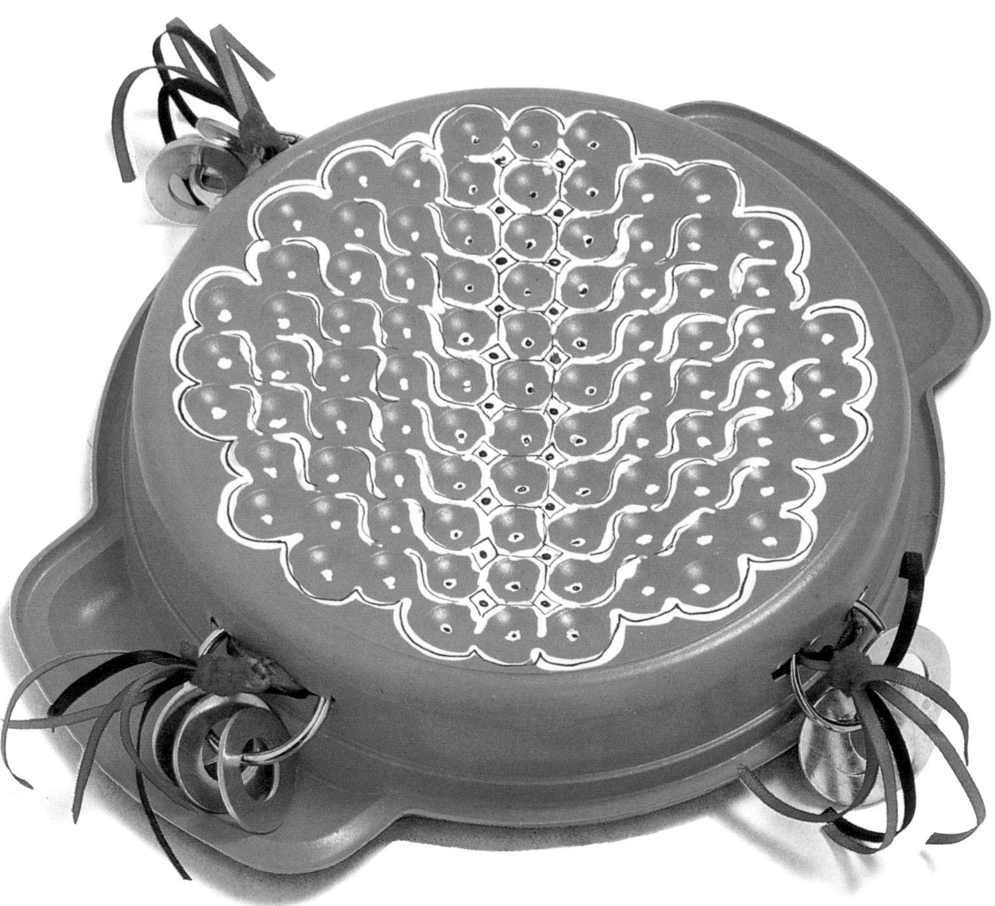

If you can find a tambourine to play, try these different playing methods:

- Hold it with one hand and hit it with the other.
- Shake it.
- Bang it against your knee or elbow.

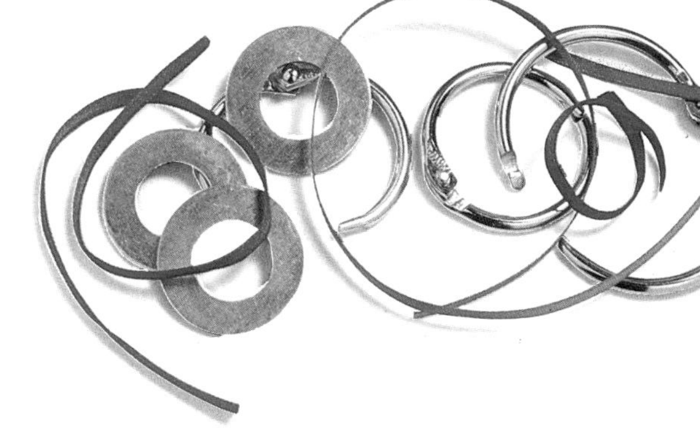

Use a paper plate!

You can make your own tambourine from a plastic or paper plate. First, cut six holes in the edge of the plate in three groups of two. Now find your jingles. You can use metal rings, buttons or balls of aluminium foil. Fix the jingles you have chosen in pairs around the edge of the plate. Decorate your tambourine with paint and ribbons and you're ready to play a lively rhythm!

The modern drum kit

A drum kit being played on stage

Wire brushes

Look at this picture of a modern drum kit. Imagine yourself playing it on stage in front of a huge audience! You walk onto the stage to the accompaniment of whistles and screams from the audience. You bend over your drums, pick up the sticks and start to play. Your hands fly in all directions as you beat the snare drum, crash the cymbals and strike a kind of drum called a tomtom. Your feet are busy too – stamping on the bass drum pedal. As you finish, exhausted, the audience jumps to its feet to applaud. You're famous!

Drummers in a rock band or jazz group need tremendous energy as well as skill. They rush from drum to drum with amazing speed. Each hand and foot seems to be doing something different, but they are all precisely in time with each other.

A diagram of a modern drum kit

The basic kit

A basic drum kit consists of a whole range of equipment. The diagram below shows you each instrument. There's a pounding bass drum, shimmering snare drum, a pair of high-pitched tomtoms and a bigger tomtom that stands on the floor. You'll probably see three kinds of cymbals, too – a hi-hat cymbal which you operate by pressing a pedal, a free-swinging crash cymbal which you hit and a more rigid ride cymbal which gives good rhythm and accent.

The next time you listen to some rock music, listen carefully to the drums. Can you tell which kind of drum is playing?

1. bass drum
2. snare drum
3. tomtom
4. hi-hat cymbal
5. ride cymbal
6. crash cymbal
7. tomtom

Recording music

A gramophone used to play music in the early 1900s

You want to listen to music played by your favourite drummer. So what do you do? You switch on a tape or CD player. But have you ever thought how the music got onto that tape or CD?

One hundred and fifty years ago, there was no recorded music at all. If you wanted to hear music you had to go to a concert or play it yourself. The earliest recordings were played on gramophones and sounded scratchy and muffled.

Music is usually recorded in a recording studio. Musicians play and sing into microphones, and these turn the sound into electric signals. The signals are registered on a multi-track tape recorder. The best recording is done digitally, which means that the electric signals are coded by a computer.

Then the engineers and performers listen to the tape and decide if any parts of the music need to be recorded again. A balance engineer can alter the balance to make sure that none of the musicians is playing too loud or too soft. You can see the range of equipment the engineers use in the picture on the next page. When everyone is happy with the recording, the tape editor cuts the tape and fits together the best parts. Then a master tape is produced.

Today, you can listen to music on a CD or DAT (Digital Audio Tape), where the sound is so realistic it is as if the musicians are playing in the room with you. Compact discs, or CDs, come from a master tape too, but this time a digitally recorded tape is used. A special beam of light called a laser beam cuts grooves into a master disc, from which the CDs are made. But don't forget that there's nothing like the excitement of hearing your favourite drummer performing at a live concert. It's hard to record atmosphere onto tape!

Recording music in the studio

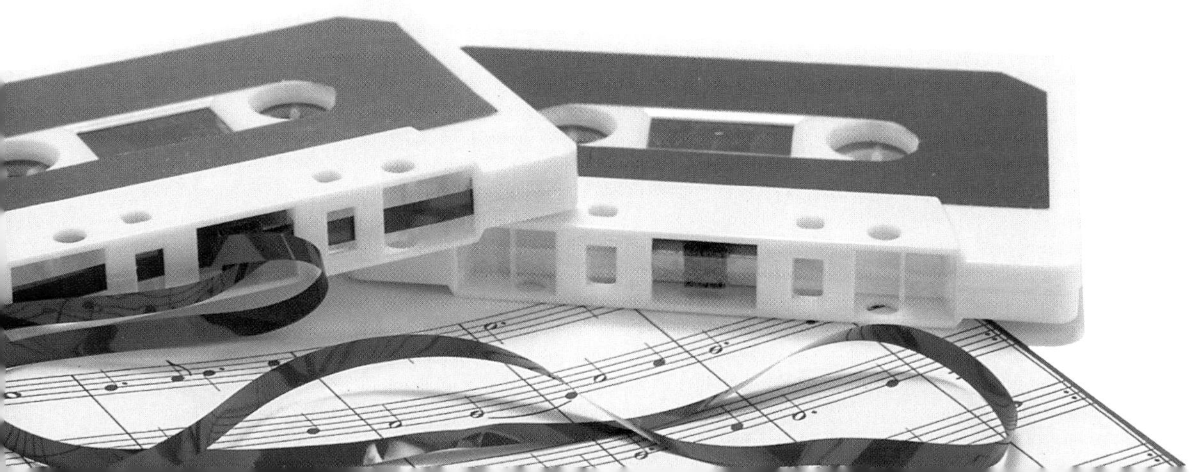

CDs and tapes

GLOSSARY OF INSTRUMENTS

barrel drum: a drum with a membrane at both ends, played on its side. Some barrel drums have only one membrane and are stood up to be played.

bass drum: the largest orchestral drum, usually hung on a frame and hit from either side. Smaller bass drums are used in marching bands.

bhaya: an Indian kettledrum. It is the left-hand drum of the tabla.

bodhran: an Irish frame drum struck with a double-headed beater called a pin.

bongos: a pair of small drums used in Latin American dance bands.

congas: a pair of barrel-shaped drums. Congas are the largest drums used in Latin American dance bands.

da-daiko: a huge drum used to play Japanese music. It is usually suspended in a frame.

darbuka: goblet drums from Islamic countries. They are usually fairly small and elaborately decorated.

eunuch flute: a mirliton found in Europe in the 1700s and 1800s.

frame drum: a drum made from one or two membranes stretched over a shallow frame.

friction drum: a drum in which the membrane is made to vibrate by friction of a cord or stick which pierces it.

goblet drum: a single-membrane drum with a goblet shape. It is an important drum in Arab countries.

kakko: a Japanese drum with two membranes. It rests on a stand and the player strikes both ends. It is used in gagaku ensembles.

kazoo: a toy mirliton. A membrane inside it vibrates when the player sings or speaks into the kazoo.

kettledrum: a drum with a single membrane stretched over a pot-shaped body. They are often played in pairs.

ko-tsuzumi: an hourglass-shaped drum with two membranes. It is held against the player's right shoulder and used to play music for the Japanese 'No' theatre.

lion roar: a friction drum that is sometimes used in orchestras. The membrane is made to vibrate with a string.

long drum: a tall, thin drum with a single membrane.

mirliton: an instrument in which the membrane vibrates to alter the sound made by speaking or singing into it.

nakers: European drums from the 1100s and 1200s. They were adapted from the Arab naqara.

naqara: a pair of small kettledrums of Arabic origin.

pellet drum: a drum made from two parts, each with a membrane covering an open end. The drum is hit with pellets tied onto string around the middle of the drum.

rommelpot: a friction drum which was popular in Europe. The membrane was made to vibrate with a stick.

side drum: a small drum with two membranes. It is played with wooden drumsticks or a wire brush.

snare drum: a side drum with two membranes. The lower membrane has strands of wire or nylon stretched over it that vibrate with the membrane to make a cracking sound.

tabla: a pair of Indian drums. It consists of a larger drum called a bhaya and a smaller one called a tabla.

talking drum: African drums used to imitate the tones of languages such as Yoruba.

tambourine: a small single-membrane drum with a frame, usually with metal disks attached to it.

timbales: similar to bongos, timbales are played in Latin American dance bands.

timpani: modern orchestral kettledrums. Timpani are tuned drums.

tsuri-daiko: a single-membrane drum which hangs from a wooden frame. It is used to play Japanese gagaku music.

vessel drum: a bowl-shaped drum with a single membrane.

waisted drum: a drum with a pinched-in waist. It can have one or two membranes.

water drum: American Indian drum made from a metal kettle covered with a single membrane. The drum is filled one-third full of water, which splashes onto the membrane.

INDEX

IMP Academy Manuscript

ACKNOWLEDGEMENTS

The publishers would like to thank the following for permission to reproduce these photographs:

Bridgeman Art Library for *Three Musicians and a Dancing Girl*, by courtesy of the Board of Trustees of the Victoria and Albert Museum (page 10); Persian musicians from *A Second Journey Through* by James Morier, British Library (pages 24-25) and *Music at the Customs House at Le Havre* by Raoul Dufy, Musée des Beaux-Arts, Le Havre/Giraudon (page 36). Clive Barda Performing Arts Library for Evelyn Glennie (page 7) and orchestral timpani (page 32). Christie's for gramophone (page 42). Collections/Roger Scruton for timpani used in Trooping the Colour (page 31). The Horniman Museum and Gardens for Nigerian talking drum (page 15) and friction drum from Zambia (page 19). Hutchison Library for Southern Indian drummer (page 4); drummer from Ghana (page 5); dancing drummers from China (page 9); drummers from Rwanda (page 12); talking drummer from Nigeria (page 14); drummers from Siberia (page 17); tabla player (page 22); da-daiko from Japan (page 29) and scene from a Japanese 'No' drama (page 29). Mansell Collection for engraving of a rommelpot player by Frans Hals (page 18). Jeremy Montagu Collection for English lion roar (page 19); French eunuch flute (page 20); pellet drum from Tibet (page 21); darbuka (page 24); European nakers (page 30); naqara (page 30); bass drum (page 37); Moroccan bendir (page 38); Japanese tambourine (page 38) and English tambourine (page 39). Tony Morrison/South American pictures for samba dancers (page 27). Premier Percussion Ltd for bass drum (page 33). Redferns for The Chieftains (page 16); drum kit (page 40) and recording studio (page 43). Sefton Photo Library for soldier marching with a snare drum (page 34).

The publishers would also like to give special thanks to Carole Mahoney and Danny Staples for their original synopsis and Tim Gray and Mickleburgh Music Shop, Bristol for the loan of musical instruments.